For Shannon

First published 2018 by Walker Books Ltd, 87 Vauxhall Walk, London SE11 5HJ

1 2 3 4 5 6 7 8 9 10

Text © 2018 Vivian French   Illustrations © 2018 Catherine Rayner

The right of Vivian French and Catherine Rayner to be identified as author and illustrator respectively of this work has been asserted by them in accordance with the Copyright, Designs and Patents Act 1988

This book has been typeset in Godlike

Printed in China

British Library Cataloguing in Publication Data: a catalogue record for this book is available from the British Library

ISBN 978-1-4063-4994-8

www.walker.co.uk

WALKER BOOKS
AND SUBSIDIARIES

LONDON • BOSTON • SYDNEY • AUCKLAND

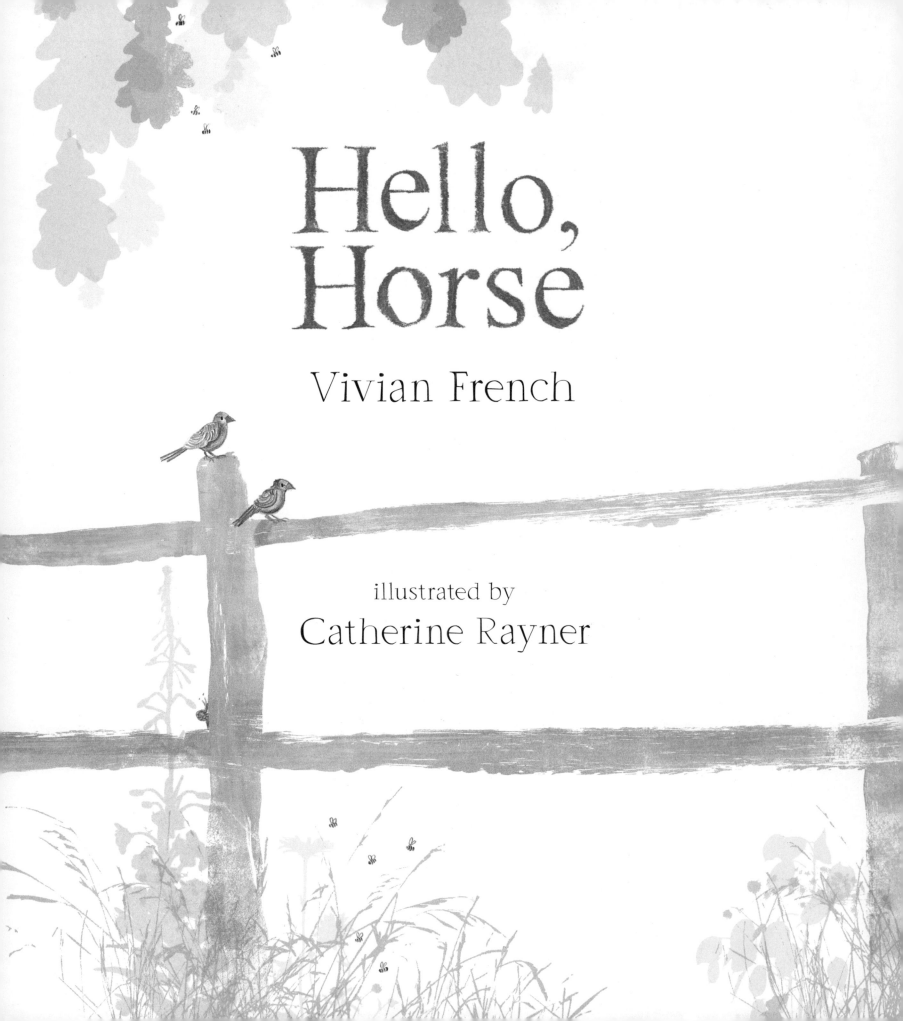

Hello, Horse

Vivian French

illustrated by

Catherine Rayner

I HAVE a friend called
Catherine, and she has
a horse called Shannon.

"Come and meet her,"
Catherine says.

I'm not sure if I like horses.

"Shannon likes people,"
Catherine tells me.

"And you'll like Shannon."

She points to a horse eating grass by the fence.

"There she is."

"She's SO big," I say.

"Shannon may look big to you, but she's very kind," says Catherine, and she calls, "Shannon! I've brought someone to meet you!"

Some horses are big and some tiny. Shannon is 15.2 hands high (about 150 cm) from her back to the ground.

Shannon throws her head up
to look at us as we walk over
to meet her. I stare at her.

She's beautiful!
Her eyes are dark, and she
looks as if she knows
everything there is to know.

Horses' eyes are either side of their heads, and
this means they can see almost all the way round.

11

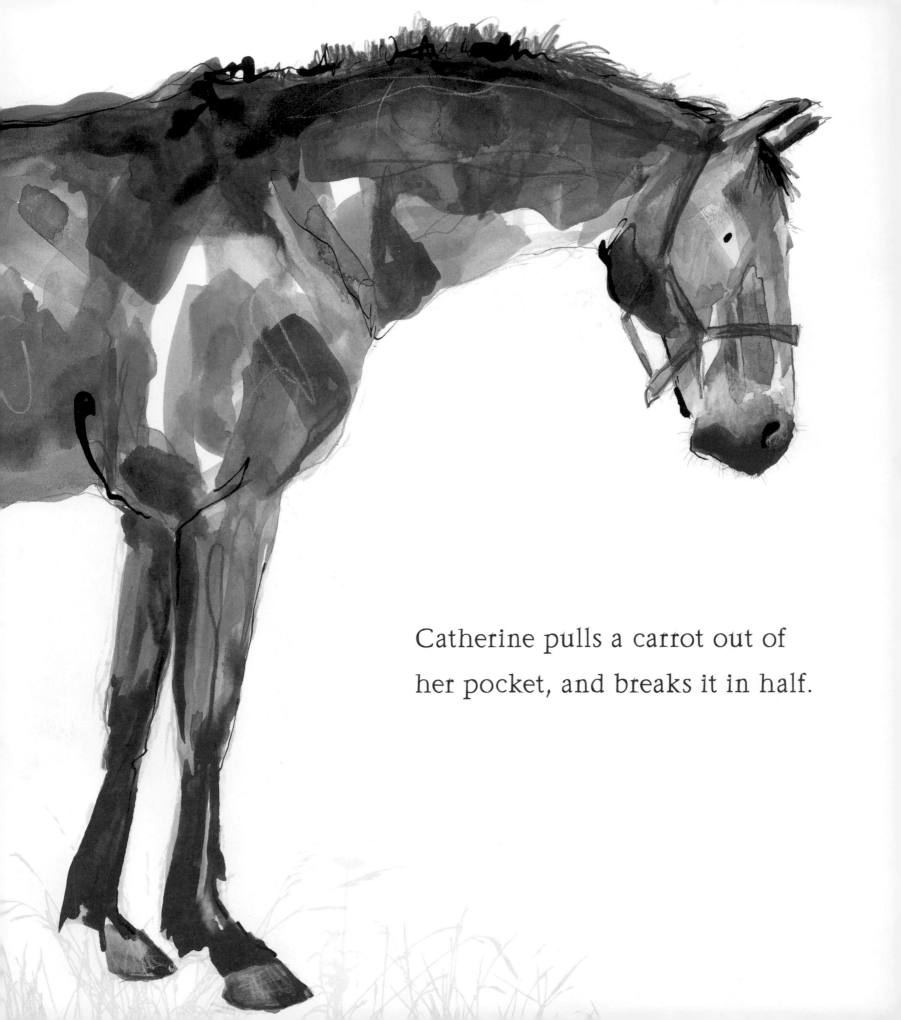

Catherine pulls a carrot out of her pocket, and breaks it in half.

"Here. Keep your hand very flat so she doesn't nibble your fingers by mistake. She won't mean to, but she can't tell where fingers end and carrot begins."

I hold out my hand, and Shannon takes the carrot. Her mouth feels just like soft velvet.

Horses are vegetarians.

"She's got VERY tickly whiskers!" I say,
and Shannon pulls her head back as if she's shocked.

"Horses have sensitive hearing."
Catherine rubs Shannon's nose.
"You have to talk quietly to
them. Would you like to
lead her to the yard?"

I feel proud leading Shannon across the field.

The ground is hard, and her feet
CLIP-CLOP as we go.

"Her feet are very noisy," I say.

"She's got metal shoes," Catherine explains.

"She wears them to protect her hooves."

Horses' hooves are like our fingernails –
they keep on growing and need regular trimming.

When we arrive at the gate, Catherine ties Shannon up.
There's a bucket full of brushes, and I watch as
Catherine chooses one.
"What are you doing?" I ask.
"I'm going to groom her. When I've brushed off all
the mud and dust, we'll put on her saddle
and bridle, and you can have a ride."

"Oh." I look at Shannon.
She puts her head down,
and looks at me.

Grooming is not only to keep the
horse clean, it's a good way to
check for cuts or injuries.

FWOOOOF!

She puffs at me through her nostrils. I feel it on my face, and it makes me laugh. "There," says Catherine. "She likes you! You can blow back ... very gently. Then she'll know you like her too."

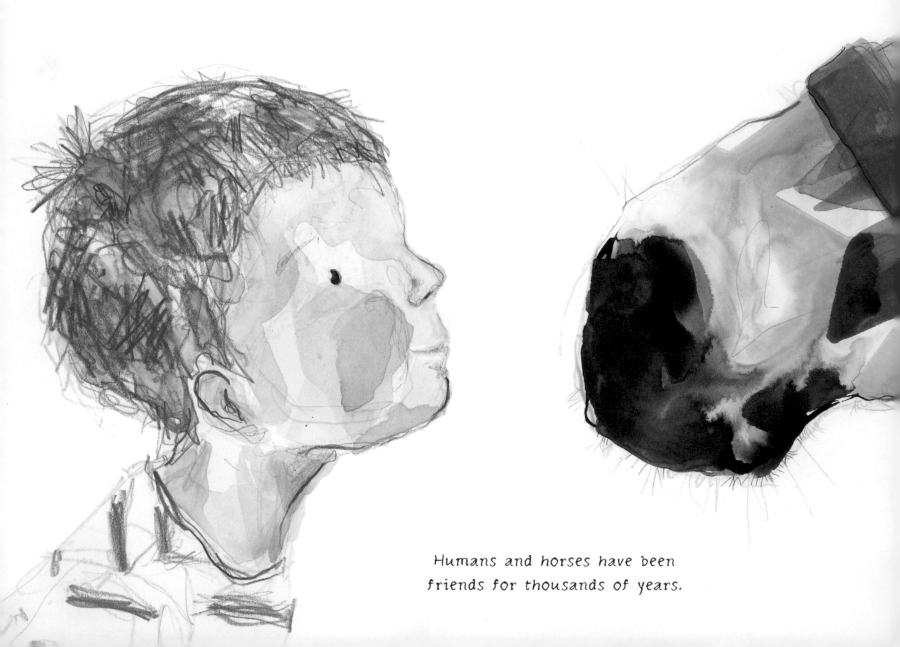

Humans and horses have been friends for thousands of years.

All the time we're talking,
Catherine is brushing Shannon,
and I can tell that she enjoys it. Even her legs get
brushed! I'd feel funny if someone brushed mine.

"All done," says Catherine and she goes to fetch the saddle and bridle.

"Um," I say, and I look at my feet. "I'm not sure I want..."

Catherine doesn't hear me. She's put on Shannon's saddle and bridle, and now she's pulling a big strap tight. "We're nearly ready," she says.

I don't say anything.

"Now," says Catherine, "time
for your first ride. Put
your foot in the stirrup."
My tummy has
butterflies, but
I do as she says.

Riders use the reins to tell the horse which way to go.

"Take hold of the reins. You can hold her mane if you feel wobbly!" Then Catherine takes my other foot, and –

25

"OH!" I say.
I'm sitting on
Shannon's back,
and it's very high up ...

It's important to always wear
a hat, in case you fall off.

and Shannon makes a funny little whickering noise.

It's as if she's saying, "Well done."

And I'm riding.

Now I have a friend called Shannon,
and Shannon has a new friend ...

me.

AUTHOR'S NOTE

When I was little I loved horses, and I still do. I did think they were very big, though, and a little bit scary...

Catherine is a real person (she's the illustrator of this book!) and Shannon is her horse. They've known each other for more than twenty years, so Shannon is very special. I met her quite a while ago, and we became friends too ... and that's what gave me and Catherine the idea for *Hello, Horse*.

Horses have been friends with people for thousands of years and, just like people, they each have their own ideas about things and their own ways of behaving. Catherine says Shannon is loyal, ticklish and sometimes pretends to be grumpy, especially when she has to come in from the field. She's always very kind to children, though ... perhaps she knows that some of them are a little bit anxious!

INDEX

Look up the pages to find out about all these horsey things. Don't forget to look at both kinds of word – **this kind** and *this kind*.

MORE INFORMATION

If you'd like to know more about horse care, try Colin Vogel's *Complete Horse Care Manual* (Dorling Kindersley, 2011).

These bits and pieces are especially useful for grooming:

body brush

hoof pick

dandy brush

mane and tail comb